Coral Snake/
Serpiente coral

By Jamie Honders   Traducción al español: Eduardo Alamán

 **Gareth Stevens**
Publishing

Please visit our website, www.garethstevens.com. For a free color catalog of all our high-quality books, call toll free 1-800-542-2595 or fax 1-877-542-2596.

Library of Congress Cataloging-in-Publication Data

Honders, Jamie.
[Coral snake. Spanish & English]
Coral snake = Serpiente coral / Jamie Honders.
   p. cm. — (Killer snakes = Serpientes asesinas)
Includes index.
ISBN 978-1-4339-5636-2 (library binding)
1. Coral snakes—Juvenile literature. I. Title. II. Title: Serpiente coral.
QL666.O64H6618 2011
597.96'44—dc22

                        2011010537

First Edition

Published in 2012 by
Gareth Stevens Publishing
111 East 14th Street, Suite 349
New York, NY 10003

Copyright © 2012 Gareth Stevens Publishing

Designer: Michael J. Flynn
Editor: Greg Roza
Spanish Translation: Eduardo Alamán

Photo credits: Cover, pp. 1, 15, 17 Michael & Patricia Fogden/Minden Pictures/Getty Images; (pp. 2–4, 6, 8, 10, 12, 14, 16, 18, 20–24 snake skin texture), p. 7 (kingsnake) Shutterstock.com; p. 5 Jim Merli/ Visuals Unlimited/Getty Images; p. 7 (coral snake) Joe McDonald/Visuals Unlimited/Getty Images; p. 9 (eastern coral snake) iStockphoto.com; p. 9 (Arizona coral snake) Gerold & Cynthia Merker/ Visuals Unlimited/Getty Images; p. 11 William Weber/Visuals Unlimited/Getty Images; p. 13 Charles Melton/Visuals Unlimited/Getty Images; pp. 18–19 Gary Meszaros/Visuals Unlimited/ Getty Images; p. 21 Michael Fogden/Photolibrary/Getty Images.

Printed in the United States of America

CPSIA compliance information: Batch #CS11GS: For further information contact Gareth Stevens, New York, New York at 1-800-542-2595.

Contents

- -

Contenido

Boldface words appear in the glossary/
Las palabras en **negrita** aparecen en el glosario

Colorful but Deadly

A coral snake is a colorful but deadly animal. It makes **venom** inside its body. The coral snake uses its **fangs** to shoot the venom into its **prey**. The venom is strong enough to kill!

Colorida y mortal

La serpiente coral es una asesina de muchos colores. La serpiente coral produce **veneno** dentro de su cuerpo. La serpiente coral usa sus **colmillos** para inyectar el veneno en su **presa**. ¡El veneno puede ser mortal!

5

Red on Yellow

Most coral snakes have black, red, and yellow bands. Many nonvenomous snakes look almost the same as the coral snake. However, only the coral snake has wide red bands between thin yellow bands.

Roja o amarilla

La mayoría de las serpientes coral tienen franjas de color negro, rojo y amarillo. Muchas serpientes que no son venenosas se parecen mucho a la serpiente coral. Sin embargo, solo la serpiente coral tienen anchas bandas rojas entre sus bandas amarillas delgadas.

king snake/
culebra reina

coral snake/
serpiente coral

7

Coral Snakes in the Unites States

Coral snakes live all over the world. They like warm areas with lots of hiding places. There are two main types of coral snakes in the United States. They are the eastern coral snake and the Arizona coral snake.

La serpiente coral en los Estados Unidos

La serpiente coral vive en todo el mundo. Estas serpientes gustan de lugares con clima templado y muchos escondites. En los Estados Unidos viven dos clases de serpientes coral. Se trata de la serpiente coral del sureste y la serpiente coral de Arizona.

Arizona coral snake/
Serpiente coral de Arizona

Eastern coral snake/
Serpiente coral del sureste

9

Adult eastern coral snakes are about 20 to 30 inches (51 to 76 cm) long. The yellow bands on this snake are often thin and dull. Some don't have yellow bands the full length of their bodies. They live in wooded, sandy, and **marshy** areas. Most are found in Florida.

La serpiente coral adulta mide de 20 a 30 pulgadas (51 a 76 cm) de largo. Las franjas amarillas de la serpiente adulta suelen ser delgadas y pálidas. Algunas no tienen franjas en el cuerpo. Estas serpientes viven en áreas arboladas, arenosas o **pantanosas**. Muchas de estas serpientes viven en la Florida.

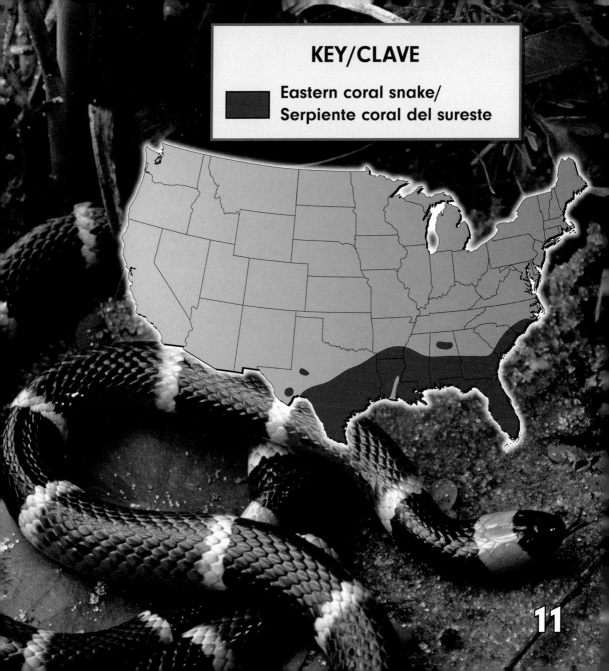

KEY/CLAVE

Eastern coral snake/
Serpiente coral del sureste

11

Arizona coral snakes are shorter and thinner than eastern coral snakes. Adults are only about 13 to 21 inches (33 to 53 cm) long. They often have brighter yellow bands than eastern coral snakes. Sometimes the bands are white instead of yellow. Arizona coral snakes like hot, dry, rocky areas.

La serpiente coral de Arizona es más corta y delgada que la serpiente del sureste. La coral de Arizona adulta mide de 13 a 21 pulgadas (33 a 53 cm) de largo. Con frecuencia sus franjas amarillas son más brillantes que las de la coral del sureste. A veces, las franjas son blancas. La serpiente coral de Arizona gusta del clima caliente y seco de las áreas rocosas.

KEY/CLAVE

Arizona coral snake/
Serpiente coral de Arizona

13

Baby Coral Snakes

Female coral snakes lay 2 to 13 eggs in summer. Then they leave the eggs. The babies break out of the eggs in 2 to 3 months. They are about 7 inches (18 cm) long. Baby coral snakes are fully venomous. They start hunting for food right away.

Serpientes coral bebé

La coral hembra pone entre 2 y 13 huevos en el verano. Luego, la coral abandona los huevos. Dos o tres meses más tarde, los bebés salen de los huevos. Tienen unas 7 pulgadas (18 cm) de largo. Los bebés son completamente venenosos. De inmediato comienzan a cazar.

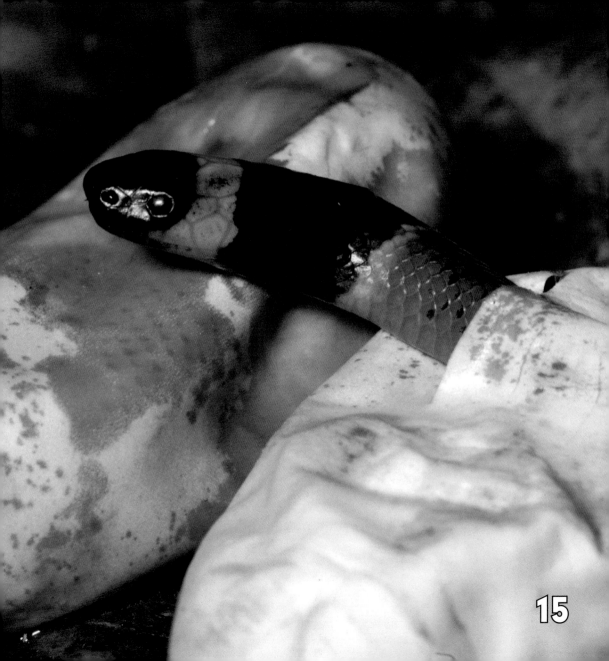

15

On the Hunt

Coral snakes eat lizards, frogs, mice, and other snakes. They hide in leaves and surprise their prey. Like other snakes, coral snakes use their tongues to smell for food. Once a coral snake bites its prey, it doesn't let go until the animal is dead.

De cacería

La serpiente de coral come lagartijas, ranas, ratones y otras serpientes. Las corales se esconden entre las hojas para sorprender a su presa. Al igual que otras serpientes, las corales usan su lengua para oler la comida. La coral no deja a su presa hasta que esta ha muerto.

Coral Snake Venom

Coral snake venom is nearly as strong as cobra venom. However, the coral snake is much smaller than a cobra. Because of this, a coral snake bite is less deadly. The venom is still strong enough to kill or **stun** small animals.

El veneno de la serpiente coral

El veneno de la serpiente coral es tan fuerte como el de la cobra. Pero la serpiente coral es más pequeña que la cobra. Es por eso que su veneno es menos mortal. Sin embargo, el veneno tiene suficiente potencia como para matar o **aturdir** a un animal pequeño.

People and Coral Snakes

Most coral snake bites happen when people step on them. A person who has been bitten by a coral snake needs to take a **medicine** called antivenin. Because of antivenin, no one in the United States has died from a coral snake bite in many years.

- -

La serpiente coral y la gente

La mayoría de las mordidas de serpiente coral se dan cuando una persona las pisa. Las víctimas de las serpientes de coral deben tomar una **medicina** llamada antídoto. Gracias a este antídoto, nadie ha muerto en muchos años en Estados Unidos por una mordida de esta serpiente.

Snake Facts/
Hoja informativa

Eastern Coral Snake/
Serpiente coral del sureste

Length/Longitud	about 20 to 30 inches (51 to 76 cm) entre 20 y 30 pulgadas (51 a 76 cm)
Colors/Colores	black, red, and yellow bands bandas negras, rojas y amarillas
Where It Lives/ Hábitat	southeastern United States sureste de los Estados Unidos
Life Span/ Años de vida	up to 7 years hasta 7 años
Killer Fact/ Datos mortales	Coral snakes have small mouths and short fangs. It's harder for them to shoot venom into prey than it is for other snakes. To make up for this, coral snakes often chew on their prey instead of just biting them! La serpiente coral tiene boca pequeña y colmillos cortos. Para la coral es difícil inyectar el veneno a su víctima. Es por eso que la coral mastica a su presa en lugar de tragársela entera.

Glossary/Glosario

fang: a long, pointed tooth

marshy: wet, soft, and muddy

medicine: a drug taken to make a sick person well

prey: an animal hunted by other animals for food

stun: to shock something so it can't move

venom: something a snake makes inside its body that can harm other animals

- -

aturdir sorprender a un animal para que no se pueda mover

colmillo (el) un diente largo y filoso

medicina (la) una droga que se le da a una persona enferma

pantanosa zona húmeda, suave y lodosa

presa (la) un animal que es cazado por otro como alimento

veneno (el) sustancia que producen las serpientes con la que pueden hacer daño a otros animales

For More Information/Más información

Books/Libros

Sexton, Colleen. *Coral Snakes.* Minneapolis, MN: Bellwether Media, 2010.

White, Nancy. *Coral Snakes: Beware the Colors!* New York, NY: Bearport Publishing, 2009.

Websites/Páginas en Internet

Eastern Coral Snake

*animals.nationalgeographic.com/animals/reptiles/
eastern-coral-snake/*
Read more about the eastern coral snake.

Western Coral Snake

www.desertusa.com/mag98/may/papr/du_westcoral.html
Read more about the western (Arizona) coral snake.

Index/Índice